IN & OUT

IN & OUT

A light hearted and personal view of what is socially
acceptable in fashionable society

Neil Mackwood

DRAWINGS BY LUCY

DUST JACKET DESIGN BY GRAHAM BISHOP

The views expressed in this work are those of
the author, and are not necessarily shared
by the publisher

DEBRETT'S PEERAGE LIMITED

Text © Neil Mackwood 1979
Illustrations © Lucy 1979
Published by Debrett's Peerage Limited
73/77 Brittania Road, London S.W.6

ISBN 0 90569 29 X

Produced by Gulliver Press Ltd

Acknowledgements

SOCIETY, like the English language, is constantly on the move but only trained observers will be aware of the changes. As Lady Elizabeth Anson has said in her Preface—for which I thank her—my task was a difficult one because no sooner had I written about a club than it changed names or decided to close or for some reason or other people vanished, got married, or died. This involved constant errata slips to the publisher and even then I was unable to keep up with the news.

Without warning Sir Charles Clore died, Lord Burghersh was no longer to be seen at his station at Wedgie's the King's Road nightclub, Lucy Clayton closed its doors as did Jackson's of Piccadilly, moves were being made to close Regine's in Kensington, Bennett in Battersea dropped down the social league table and was taken over while L'Escapade and The English House became fashionable places to eat; Baron Bentinck's Boulevard magazine ceased to appear on the more esoteric London news stands and the Earl of Snowdon's new wife gave birth to Frances.

But if my task was a daunting one it has been made easier by the help of many friends who have passed advice and criticism and have helped compile the lists—although I do not shirk from my responsibility as the author. I would like to pass on my special thanks to Nigel Dempster, who by employing me after I tapped him on the shoulder at Ascot, made the book possible and it must be said he paved the way with his own list of INs and OUTs earlier in the year although, to save being called a plagiarist, I would add this book was by then under way. Another former colleague Tully Potter lent me his tremendous knowledge of music and Christopher Allen and Philip Townsend helped in other areas. Douglas Sutherland, no stranger to the House of Debrett, I thank for telling me about rivers — in which he spends so much of his time. Finally my parents who lent me their country house when the distractions of London kept me from my typewriter — a sincere thank you and to Catherine Clancy who so resolutely stood beside me for several years while I indulged in vigorous field research.

N.F.M.
Burwash, August 1979.

Contents

Preface

FOR the last 19 years I have run my business Party Planners and I can appreciate how difficult it is to keep up with what is IN and OUT because so much can change between the planning of a party and its execution. One band, which may have been fashionable at the time of booking, may not be so sought after six months later. So I have every sympathy with the author who must have spent much of his time amending his manuscript in order to keep up with the changing fashions. After all, in the lapse of time between the conception of the book and its publication the scene may have changed so much that what he decided was very much IN may now be very much OUT. Last year it might have been IN to be seen eating out, and this year it might be IN to be discovered eating at home.

For this reason I feel those people or places that find themselves on the OUT-side should not despair, and those on the IN-side should not throw their hats in the air. As for those unlucky enough not to be mentioned at all, they must remain hopeful. They should be bold and endeavour to feel confident that they will be on the IN-side, next year.

Although I hope the author did not take his formidable task too seriously (or he might have ended up IN-sane and OUT-cast) his book could prove to be an interesting insight about the way of life in 1979-80 for our children and grandchildren to enjoy. I am certain they will hardly believe that it was once possible to have a shoe or shirt hand-made. It will illustrate to them just how ephemeral fashionable life is.

LADY ELIZABETH ANSON

Introduction

SOCIETY has been defined as being a more or less permanent group of people living together and sharing a common way of life, attitudes and beliefs. But the word 'society' conjures up a picture of a privileged section of our community, who assemble together in exclusive surroundings to banter wittily with each other, as a kind of diversion from life. For years it has remained a mystery as to who are the members of this élite club whose hedonistic pursuits are sometimes presented in the gossip columns for the delectation of the proletariat.

Increasing egalitarianism in this, a socialist democracy, has opened up the doors of what was once an impregnable fortress—with the keyholders coming from the ranks of royalty, the aristocracy, landed gentry and an occasional artist like Oscar Wilde.

While society—I talk of the young contemporary sort whose headquarters is London—now welcomes new blood, the old social pitfalls remain. Prospective members have to plot their course through a social minefield and at every turn the new boy (the parvenu) runs the risk of being exposed and cast out.

The old guard—in the form of their offspring—remains and it is an undeniable fact that old money wins out over new. However, just as some French clarets with famous names need bolstering with Italian wine, society in the seventies is bound to accept new arrivals who have something to lend it.

This may be a lively wit—always in demand—a trade (photography), money acquired, maybe, from the manufacture of blue jeans or cutting hair, a ravishing figure, a pretty face or an unquestionable drive to have fun.

The would-be social athlete has to be on his guard, for society can be a viper's nest of bitchery. This book is directed partly to the hopeful candidate and is presented as my personal guide to what is socially acceptable, and more important, what is not. It is to be used as a mine detector for those brave enough to traverse the minefield.

NEIL MACKWOOD

1

Birth

IT IS not important where to be born but the smartest place remains at home, largely because the medical services are dead against it.

IN	OUT
At home	In the back of a cab
St. Mary's, Paddington	Alfresco
(favoured by royalty)	BUPA assisted
Queen Charlotte's	Aboard the QE2
In flight on Concorde	

Choice of Names

Parents can damage a child's mind by calling their son Hercules or their daughter Hyacinth. Although it is difficult to stand up philosophically, names do have a class ring to them. A Charles and Edwina are more likely to come from the higher socio economic class than a Doris and Fred who are very likely to be 'mine hosts' at The Dog and Duck—although Princess Michael of Kent has re-introduced a Frederick to the royal family. Choose carefully—and if your parents have not there is always the deed poll.

Children's Names

Boys

IN	OUT
Charles	Sidney
Michael	Lew
David (never Dave)	Bernard
Robert (not Bob)	Algernon
Niall	Nigel

DESMOND

Marc	Jasper
Adnan	Harold
Dickie	Tarquin
Andrew	Patrick/Paddy
Geoffrey	Jeremy
Rory	Pearson
Adam	Kenneth
Christopher	Winston
Auberon	Clive
Bruno	Chapman
Julian	Eric
Pierre	Oscar
Sam	Montagu
Hugh	Dennis
Anthony (not Tone)	Rod
Constantine	Idi
Edward	
Rupert	
Ned	

Girls

IN	OUT
Emily	Shirley
Melanie	Erica
Victoria	Esther
Catherine	Joan
Diana	Beatrice
Sally	Doris
Lucy	Dolly
Susannah	Francesca
Margaret	Petula
Elizabeth	Diane
Sophie	Imogen
Lucinda	Florence
Flora	Rosaline
Davina	Rebecca

(2)

. . . "found the stupid girl trying to put the poor little
chap in the washing machine."

Camilla	Emerald
Debbie	Mary
Daphne	Daisy
Leila	Audrey
Barbara	Barbra
Tara	Ernestine
Georgina	Georgiana
Lyndall	Tamsin
Anoushka	Sandra
Amanda	Dee
Angie/Angela	Bianca

Au Pairs

Rather like the Greek Islands which were smart before Dan Air arrived on the scene, Au Pairs are more than a little demode. Recently they have been introduced to that interminable story of country-folk, The Archers — which proves the point.

Au Pairs in fact are nothing but trouble — either your best friend or husband runs off with them or they create havoc at home. Young wives love to bring out their au pair disaster stories.

"Helga brought this terrible looking car dealer back home with her last night — and I have warned her about having men in her room. She can do what she wants in the park but not under my roof" . . . . or: "Can you imagine I told Mimi to wash the baby and when I got back I found the stupid girl trying to put the poor little chap into the washing-machine".

The English nanny — dependable, kind if a little strict, and expensive has returned to fashion. Jonathan Gathorne Hardy's 'The Rise and Fall of the British Nanny' is already out of date.

Nannies	*Au Pairs*
IN	OUT
Norland	All

Bars with optics, pub mirrors at home — OUT

Albemarle
Princess Christian
Knightsbridge
Nannies Kensington

The home environment

IN	OUT
Flying ducks (inverted chic)	TV games
	Chiming door bells
Cord carpets (so practical)	Shag pile carpets
Fish tanks (not goldfish)	Garden sculptures
Wallpaper (not Laura Ashley)	Gnomes
	G-plan
Pine kitchens	TV security cameras
Entry-phones	Front doors with peepholes
Mahogany front doors	
Bidets	Round baths
Ceefax and Oracle	Bars with optics, pub mirrors, electric carving knives

Pets to have at Home

Dogs

IN	OUT
Old English Sheepdogs (Bobtails)	Greyhounds (not racing)
	Whippets
Boxers	Corgis
Pugs	Otter Hounds
Cavaliers	Fox Hounds (not hunting)
Great Danes	Alsatians
Battersea canines	Chihuahuas
Weimeranas	Labradors (yellow)
Labradors (black)	Jack Russells
Shar-Pei (very ugly but very rare)	Red Setters
	Poodles (except standard)
English Setters	Cocker Spaniels

(6)

Dalmatians (pretty but
    silly)
Springer Spaniels
Pointers
Salukis

Pekinese (not the cooking)
Rhodesian Ridgebacks

Other Pets

IN	OUT
Geese	Caged birds (except
Ducks	Harewood bird garden)
Doves	Racing Pigeons
Goldfish (in ponds only)	Goldfish (tanks)
Chickens	Grass snakes
Bush Babies	Frogs
Monkeys	Snakes
Hamsters (very U)	Mice, rats
Guinea Pigs	Tortoises
Rabbits (children only)	Gerbils
Donkeys	
Horses	
Goats	

Cats

IN	OUT
Burmese	Blotched domestics
Siamese	Tabbies
Persians (white and black)	Manx (striped or white)
Strays	Manul or Pallas's Cats
Abyssinians	

2

Schooling

WHILE it is anathema to most Americans to pack their kinder off to boarding school seven or eight years after their birth it is second nature to the British upper classes to send their children off to the draughty, austere workhouses known as Public Schools. The best joke of all is to send their offspring to the school their parents were made to endure, regardless of the horrors they had to suffer at the hands of sadistic masters or bullies.

Public schools became terribly unfashionable in the sixties and graduates from the system dropped their 'stand-up-for-ladies-when-they-come-into-a-room' manners and swopped their plumby tones for a more socially acceptable mid-Atlantic intonation or a Home Counties twang.

But since the days of flower power the public school has returned to fashion and young men and women once again boast that they were schooled at Rugby, Ampleforth or Gordonstoun. The socially insecure and potentates from India, Africa and the Middle East — who love to send their turbaned offspring to an English public school — have ensured the continuation of the system which Socialism has tried to dissolve.

While the ex-public schoolboy is once again recognisable, with his quaint fondness for spotted cravats, scarves with the old place's colours and, above all, that all-boys-together mateyness, the potential socialite need have no fear if he was educated at Kettering Grammar School and at a university described as being Red Brick. There are dodges.

The ex p.s. boy loves to brag about how terrible it all

was. "My glass of water used to freeze over when I left it on the windowsill overnight" is a favourite. Drinking stories (c.f. Prince Charles and the cherry brandy) predominate, as do tales about non-existent conquests. But fagging, now being phased out in some more enlightened schools, is a topic which old boys talk of fondly.

"My first task at Charterhouse was to warm the bog (lavatory) seat for a prefect" or, "I had to light Tomlinson's fire in his study, clean his shoes and put out a new collar before waking him with a pot of china tea", are typical examples. The climber, lucky enough not to have been sent to p.s., just has to learn a few such details.

The resourceful Nigel Dempster (Sherborne), before he embarked on his successful career as a social watcher/climber joined the city and realised that deals would come quicker if he could somehow identify himself with the backgrounds of the people he was dealing with. Before a meeting he would ascertain which school his victim had attended — and would appear in the appropriate old school tie. "I never knew you went to Fettes," — a quick change of subject after affirmation and the deal would sail through.

A word about Eton — above all the school to which the socially ambitious will send their sons in the mistaken belief that they will get a leg-up. Eton, which someone said was too close to London and too far removed from reality, has perhaps been overtaken in status by Gordonstoun — thanks to Royal patronage. Nevertheless the school attracts a fair share of the sons of the peerage and paradoxically a large proportion of parvenus.

Old Etonians themselves are tremendous snobs, as is illustrated by the true story of two of their kind who were guests at one of Her Majesty's closed houses. Both inmates had succeeded in getting jobs in the library and were talking together about old times when the curiosity of another 'guest' was aroused. Hearing the unmistakable

"I was at St. Paul's"

tones of the Public School he approached timidly and proffered the information: "I was at St. Paul's." After swopping glances one Old Etonian looked towards the intruder and said: "I should keep very quiet about that if I were you."

To save entrants (either to society or public school) from resorting to the advice of Gabbitas-Thring here is a list of IN and OUT schools.

Preparatory Schools
Boys

IN	OUT
Ludgrove	Durlston Court
Horris Hill	Neville Holt
Colet Court	Hailybury Jnr
The Dragon School	Heatherdown
Eaton House	Ashdown House
Cheam	
Stoke Brunswick	

Public Schools

IN	OUT
Ampleforth (for left footers)	Stowe
	Bryanston
Westminster	Canford
Eton	Bradfield
Harrow	Oundle
Charterhouse	Lancing
Gordonstoun	Tonbridge
Holland Park Comprehensive (almost)	Brighton College
	St. Paul's
Winchester (for swots)	Mill Hill
Malvern	Haileybury
Rugby	Clayesmore
Radley	
Shrewsbury	
Milton Abbey	

Preparatory Schools
Girls
All out. Young ladies should remain at home to be taught the social graces such as how to sit, walk, converse and conduct themselves in public. If shoved off to boarding school before puberty, girls develop an unhealthy heartiness which can be very costly to erase—usually at finishing school in Switzerland. Unfortunately, such an education rarely teaches a young lady basic arithmetic or how to spell.

Girls Public Schools

IN	OUT
Bedgebury Park	Benenden
Heathfield	Godolphin
Cobham Hall	Sherborne
Roedean	Croft House
Cheltenham Ladies College	Queens Gate
Francis Holland	St. Mary's, Ascot
Convent of the Holy Child, Mayfield (for left footers)	Southover
West Heath	

Higher education
Although the dedicated climber will be longing to make his assault on society, it is true that a spell at either Oxford or Cambridge will do him no harm—as long as he learns early to mix with the right sort of undergraduate and joins clubs like The Pitt which is dedicated to hedonism and snobbery. Provincial universities, with a few exceptions, are only good for toning-up the intellectual muscles and learning how to be a computer pro-

grammer or such things as dealing with traffic flows. Later in this book I shall be talking about subjects which the diligent climber should know about — wine, manners, eating out, etc.

IN	OUT
Rada (Royal Academy of very Dramatic Arts)	Brunel
	Essex
Inchbald School of Design	Buckingham
Royal College of Art	Manchester
Open University	New University of Ulster
University of Dublin Trinity College	Queen's University, Belfast
St. Andrew's	Heriot-Watt University
Oxford except Brasenose, St. Catherine's, University and St. Hilda's colleges)	Newcastle
	Hull
	Exeter
	Birmingham
Cambridge except Clare (too brainy)	Warwick
	Sheffield
Fitzwilliam, Selwyn and Wolfson colleges	Reading
	East Anglia
London School of Economics	Salford
	Surrey
Harvard	Bradford
York	Durham (v. churchy)
Sussex	London
Leeds	
Keele (for lefties)	
Kent	

3
Jobs

WITHIN living memory it was quite unfashionable to work, or at least to be in the employ of anyone else. If you were the heir it was expected that you would run the estate, but if one was born to be the second or third son the army and church would have been acceptable 'callings'.

Until the silicone chip makes us all redundant it is now wholly fashionable to work for a living rather than to rely on the family trust to provide the necessary. This applies equally to both sexes.

To pursue ones hedonistic nature by not earning a living produces feelings of guilt and arouses suspicion in those who trudge to offices every day.

The work ethic, so unfashionable between the war years, is back but jobs must be sought which will add to your interest. Announce the fact that you are an accountant and people will doubtless feign interest while they shoot glances over your shoulder in the direction of the film director. Say that you are a computer programmer and people will leave your company in droves in search of a poet or publisher who will have interesting things to say about his work.

To be a housewife is 'out' unless one is in the process of bearing or rearing small children. Talk about nappy rash and colic is not of universal interest but a mother who goes out to work is now 'in'.

Whereas in the past daughters stayed at home to help mother entertain or engaged themselves in charity work, they are now encouraged to find work outside the family nest.

. . . the familiar twang of Cheltenham Ladies' College
can now be heard backstage at the National.

One girl—the poor thing would have had the debutante season to concentrate on had she been born five years earlier—told me that her mother was anxious that she get a good job at somewhere like Harrods. (I always did wonder what all those girls with plumby accents were doing serving behind the counter of the headscarf department).

Rather than rush into marriage at an unsuitable age, girls who would have been at home helping out at the Conservative Fête are now shifting scenery, being journalists, interior designers and auctioneers, or learning the Montessori method of teaching. The twang, more familiar to the playing fields of Cheltenham Ladies' College, can now be heard emanating from the television news to backstage at the National Theatre.

Of course the trick is to seek a job which not only pays well, but satisfies an interest and makes you more fascinating to others. Thus Nigel Dempster has got a job which fulfils his need to social climb and influence, the Earl of Lichfield and the Earl of Snowdon are paid vast sums for what was their hobby (photography), Mr. David Somerset, the heir presumptive to the Duke of Beaufort, is a fine art dealer, Lord Hesketh ran a Grand Prix team and still has interests in cars, Viscount St. Davids satisfies his interest by running a canal boat company and the gourmet Viscount Newport runs the Caviar Bar and Porters in Covent Garden.

Gentlemen know more about the land than anything else and have always had the knack of finding jobs to entertain their interest—such as working for The Game Conservancy who employ them to count the number of grouse shot every season. Or they get elected to the Jockey Club and indulge their interest in racing. Douglas Bunn started his own show jumping complex, as did Mr. George Lane Fox at Bramley Park in Yorkshire.

Given a choice most land-loving gentlemen would love

Counting the number of grouse shot.

to be gamekeepers or gillies and secretly envy the people they employ in this position.

The rise in society of hairdressers, designers etc. is due to vanity. As has been said, society reveres beauty and anyone who can help it in that aim has, at this moment, a place, but I suspect the appeal will be a transitory one.

To be a pop-singer in the seventies is not the generally insane experience it was in the late sixties, although the aristocracy still appear delighted when one of their daughters marries a songster (c.f. Lady Sophia Crichton-Stuart, daughter of the Marquess of Bute and Jimmy Bain of the Wild Horses group) — because the least it can do is bring in more money to the family.

for the girls

IN	OUT
Photographer	Secretary
Art Restorer	Receptionist
P.R.	Go-go dancer
Musician	Stockbroker
Ballet dancer	Commodity broker
Actress	Charity worker
Speech therapist	Parliamentary worker
Don	Teacher
Designer (interior, dress, jewellery, graphic)	Masseuse
	Nurse
Journalist	Florist
Novelist	Dog breeder
TV, radio reporter	Horse groom
Doctor	Model (photographic)
Model (fashion)	To hunt full time
Artist	Vet
Sculptor	Chauffeuse
Bookbinder	Cooking directors' lunches

Antique dealer
Glass blower
Rose grower
Potter
TV and film make-up
   artist
Prime Minister

Market gardener
Mechanic
Air hostess (and any other
   kind)
Hairdresser
Beautician

for the boys

IN	OUT
Anything in oil	Commercial airline pilot
Publishing	Vet
Restaurateur	Chef (except in France)
Anything in wine	Hotelier
Christies	Sotheby's
Farming	Tailor
Journalist	Milliner
Interior designing	Shopkeeper
Furniture designing	Modelling
Architect	Banking
Land agent	Ship broking
Genealogist	Commodity broking
Rock singer	Accountancy
Record producer	Agronomist
Film producer	TV cameraman
Film cameraman	Fine art dealer
Photographer	Doctor
TV, radio reporter	Dentist
Cosmetic surgeon	Stock broker
Playwright	Golf professional
Theatre	Jeweller
director/impresario	Sales representative
Ship's captain	Politician
Pyschologist	Foreign office worker
Trichologist	
Theatrical agent	

The Forces

Having decided to become a dedicated climber the subject will have little time for diversions. He cannot risk
being posted to the Rhine or Hong Kong (out), Belize. He
must remain in the centre of things and not be keeping
the mosquitoes at bay in Belize.

One prominent Peer was quoted (he later denied the
quote) that the only avenue in life where class distinction
was thriving was the Army. But if our social athlete feels
it is his duty to follow Daddy into the Army here are some
of the regiments he must apply to.

IN

The Household Cavalry;
  The Blues and Royals,
  The Life Guards—
  known as the Picadilly
  Cowboys. (The dis-
  advantage of joining
  these regiments is that
  while you are galloping
  up and down the Mall
  tourists can make life
  unbearable—and there
  is no form of retaliation
  other than a windy
  horse).
The SAS (for the climber
  who prefers to scale
  mountains rather than
  the social ladder)
Scots Guards (for the
  uniform)
Coldstream and Grenadier
  Guards

Greenjackets (for fast
  movers).
Royal Horse Artillery.

If Barbara Cartland (out) is to be believed, the man in a
uniform has a better chance of attracting the female eye,
but this is the stuff of romantic novels. It is a provincial
idea which has no sway with the urbane climber who
realises there are easier ways of ingratiating his way into
the company of females.

One successful climber of my acquaintance who
entered the dangerous realm of gossip columns and lost
all his 'friends' took the unusual step of joining the police.
This can be seen as a light-hearted jape and only added
to his social interest. At the time he was the only
policeman to be a member of Annabel's and could
delight his friends with racy stories of the low life he
encountered. For my part, I believe he joined the con-
stabulary not to enhance his social interest, but to learn
the workings of the police—how to avoid parking fines
and the like.

Charities

Enhance social position by working for:-	Better left to others:-
Action Research for the Crippled Child	Oxfam
Gunnar Nilson Cancer Fund	Amnesty International
NSPCC	Save the Children
Retired Gentlefolk's Association	RSPCA
Red Cross	Shelter
Lepra	Printers Charitable Trust
Cancer Research Fund Imperial	UNICEF
The Samaritans	National Trust
	National Festival of Light
	Cyrenians
	Barristers Benevolent Association

War on Want
Chelsea Physic Garden
Royal National Institute
    for the Deaf
Child Poverty Action
    Group

. . . . : "like man you know."

4

Language

CLASSLESS accents have replaced the Oxford drawl of Noel Coward's day, except it can be heard emanating from the mouths of those who have attended too many elocution classes. Thus regard with scepticism the person who talks of gels (girls), goff (golf), dashing orf (rushing off) and Cod (as in oh God!). He/she is trying too hard to be U. With the arrival on the scene of interior decorators, hairdressers, actors, models, tradesmen posing as shop-keepers, sportsmen, pop-singers, photographers, journal-ists, night-club owners, restaurateurs, exotics and dress designers, the upper-middle class haw-haw tones have been eroded by nasal northern, cockney and home counties twangs. It remains an advantage to speak with-out an accent unless, like Janet Street-Porter, it is your trademark. Above all, in contemporary society the glib are admired — the articulate win out over those who have the diction of a footballer. The 'like-man-you-know' phraseology of the sixties has once again given way to those who can express themselves and amuse with their utterances.

People who do not speak the Queen's English
like she speaks it

Russell Harty (northern)
Melvyn Bragg (nasal northern)
Michael Parkinson (northern)
Sir Harold Wilson (northern)
Edward Heath (southern)
David Frost (home counties)
Alan Whicker (home counties)

John Lloyd (home counties)
Janet Street-Porter (cockney)
Pat Booth (cockney)
Twiggy (cockney)
Lorraine Chase (cockney)
Terence Stamp (home counties)
Jean Rook (northern)
Colin Welland (northern)
Mynah Bird (exotic)
Johnny Speight (cockney)
Peter Langan (Irish)
Austin Mitchell (northern)
Freddy Laker (home counties)
Victor Matthews (cockney)
Larry Lamb (northern)
Larry Adler (foreign)
Arianna Stassinopoulos (foreign)
Luis Sosa Basualdo (foreign)
Charles Riachi (foreign)
Homayoun Mazandi (foreign)
David Hockney (northern)
Ram (exotic)
Clive James (antipodean)
Angie Bowie (foreign)
Clive Jenkins (Welsh perhaps)

Passé and out words/expressions

far out
hassle
like man . . .
right on
you know
heavy (applied to a situation)
squeeze a tube (Australian vulgarity)
acid
at this moment in time

weekend

get it together

vibes

skirt, bird, doll, moll, old lady (meaning girls)

old bean, handsome, matey (as terms of endearment between males)

cool

radio (wireless is coming back)

to score (in the sexual sense 'boffing' is in vogue)

courting — use stepping out

give me a bell — use telephone

dinner suit — use dinner jacket

home — say house or chez Nigel

smokes — use cigarette

condiments, cruets — use salt and pepper

cutlery — use knives and forks

toilet, men's room, powder room — use loo or lavatory

posh — use smart

hoi polloi — snobs say oikes or the lower orders

apartment — flat is better, or duplex

cheers — as a form of greeting ignore it and when applied to a toast say 'Good health'

the filth, pigs, bluebottles, old Bill, the law as applied to the police are underworld expressions — use coppers

lounge — sitting room unless at an airport

bubbly — say champagne

abroad — say overseas

the flicks — films

bathing — use swimming

wheels — use either car or motorbike

tired and emotional is an over used Private Eye expression — use 'in his cups' or 'irrational'

shaking a leg — use bopping

coming out — an old debutante (out) term now applied to homosexuals

pants — an Americanism for trousers

(27)

no way (overworked)

get your act together (USA usage)

give me the bottom line (cut it short)

get the show on the road (overworked circus expression)

clones

too much

do you dig (nothing to do with gardening but a quaint 50's phrase)

lay it on me (music business jargon)

have a good day (strictly Stateside)

scribbler (journalist)

hi-fi (say record player or gramophone if you have one)

disc (record)

kind of freaked out and my mind was blown (USA usage)

hotshot

hippy, dropout

let's split (go our separate ways)

let's crash (go to sleep)

I am vacationing (on holiday)

a whole new ball game (an American baseball game expression)

to be laid back (something they specialise in in Los Angeles, presumably because it is too hot, but it means to be nonchalant)

good vibes (nothing to do with Lionel Hampton but an outdated sixties expression)

situation

5

People

PEOPLE collect people just as the National Gallery collects important works of art. It is an exercise of mutual benefit. People — well certain types of people — are what society is about. It is an undeniable fact (almost) that the contents of Debrett's Peerage (pre 1914) know each other — thus the nobility have an advantage over lesser mortals who do not share the common bond of breeding.

Society consists of smaller groups, the polo set, the hunting set (out), politicos, media people, the racing fraternity and more recently the new wave of hairdressers, interior decorators, singers and actors. The Chelsea set, if it ever existed, does not now.

To obtain an IN the person who hankers after recognition must learn the cast list. This involves the seeking out of various key figures who are in the position to advance your status either by inviting you to places where you will have a chance to sparkle (or fall from grace) or to sponsor you as a promising new arrival. New blood is constantly sought to revive the body.

Going about this exercise in the wrong way will expose the climber for what he is and that will close the door on him for ever. To be seen cultivating is as much social suicide as to admit a loathing for horses.

The spreading about of vast wads of money is unwise. Apart from inducing an undesirable state of bankruptcy it will quickly have the old school raising quizzical eyebrows, although, it must be said they do enjoy the munificence of the donor with open arms and mouths.

The best method of infiltration is by osmosis — a gentle process of absorption. Having learnt who the players of

People collect people

the game are and where they are to be found having fun, the trick is simply to BE AROUND. This involves following the social calendar: Winter Sports in Gstaad, The Rose Ball (out), the Monaco Grand Prix, The Derby which is a useful trial run for Ascot, The Berkeley Square Beano, Cowes Week and Goodwood. Important premiers must be taken in: The Royal Academy Summer Show, Opera and Theatre openings; get invited to public and private parties. Such endurance will ensure that you are noticed — although existing members (especially new arrivals keen to guard their status) may not let on that you are a contender. All the time your face will be becoming more familiar.

Versatility is a vital asset. The more dedicated climber must be equally at home chatting to dripping polo players at Smith's Lawn (treading-in is an excellent arena for new introductions and Prince Charles is often in evidence) or discussing horseflesh with Lord Howard de Walden and Porchy at the Newmarket November sales.

In his/her contacts book (it is not only journalists who keep them) will be a high court judge, a churchman, a prominent barrister, a coterie of millionaires or land-owners with houses suitable for Friday until Monday parties, a smattering of arts people, including a singer, author and artist, a sympathetic hostess, as many titles as can be mustered, some paid persuaders, an owner of a shoot, a city figure, a restaurant and nightclub proprietor and a giggle of playboys.

Just as newboys at the more traditional public schools (prisons?) are encouraged, with the threat of torture if they fail to learn the names of hundreds of strangers in a matter of weeks, the social athlete must commit all the names and faces to the index of his mind.

Come Ascot week he or she will recognise 'everyone' who comes through the gates and will not be forced to drop their gaze to the lapel — where is pinned the punter's

(31)

name. Ascot remains the one institution, apart from the Army, which is a bastion of class consciousness. Here the lower middle class and working classes can pretend to be what they are not. Everyone looks important in their hired rig, binocular cases with old race-meeting tickets dangling, and seemingly knowledgeable comments pencilled in on the race-card.

It is a time to make an impression. "Sonia and Hugh are looking so happy," or "Robert and Susan have just got back from America" or better still "Old Halifax says to have a nibble at No. 4 in the 3.30".

Some Nobility

For the purposes of this book nobility is IN. If titles do not have the same pull as they did for the last generation they still count for a lot. Increasing egalitarianism has placed many formerly rich peers in the ranks of the hardly well off — although England's richest man is probably the new Duke of Westminster, who owns 300 acres of Mayfair and Belgravia (i.e. London) and much more besides.

Whereas in the past when the *status quo* was generally a matter of acceptance by all classes, the ranks of the nobility have been brought within reach of the middle classes.

Thus the Marquis of Queensberry teaches pottery, Lord Burghersh used to greet guests in a London nightclub when not competing on the Winter slopes, Viscount Newport plays host at his Caviar Bar Restaurant and The Earl of Harewood supplements his living by running the English National Opera.

With four Royal and 26 other Dukes, 38 Marquesses, 199 Earls, 131 Viscounts, 487 barons and 20 peeresses to choose from, I present a personal list as a guide of those who I feel are more conducive to the blandishments of the orders below themselves.

Dukes
Bedford
Buccleuch
Marlborough (for his offspring and an invitation to the family seat)
Norfolk (has excellent shooting in Yorkshire and pretty daughters)
Roxburghe
Westminster

Marquesses
Bath
Granby
Bute
Hartington
Tavistock
Milford Haven
Northampton
Queensberry
Blandford (the leader of the set for the early 80's)
Londonderry

Earls
Dalkeith
Jermyn (he will not be around London for a while)
Dumfries
Rocksavage
Alexander of Tunis
Cawdor
Lichfield
Denbigh
Normanton
Pembroke (as Henry Herbert he makes films)
Suffolk and Berkshire
Arundel

Viscounts, Barons and bearers of courtesy titles

Lord Seymour

Lord Rupert Nevill

Viscount Weymouth (still a hairy Wessex Regionalist)

Viscount Erleigh

Lord Greenock

Viscount Lewisham

Viscount Moore (a photographer)

Lord Irwin

Viscount Lascelles (a film maker)

Viscount Petersham

Viscount Brocas

Viscount Stormont (one to watch)

Viscount Windsor (nothing to do with the Royal Family)

Lord Burghersh

Viscount Norwich

Viscount Portman

Viscount Rothermere

Viscount Soulbury (a Hindu monk)

Lord Bethell

Lord Hesketh (less of a party-boy since marriage)

Lord Melchett

Lord Montagu of Beaulieu

Lord Tryon

Lord Vestey

Lord David Dundas

Lord Camoys (of Stonor Park at last)

Lord Feversham (mainly to be found tramping his Yorkshire estate)

Lord Harlech

Lord Henley

Lord Ogilvy

*Ex-kings, members of the most exclusive club in the
world*

Simeon of Bulgaria (Madrid)

Reghad of Tunisia (London/Paris)
Umberto of Italy Portugal)
Michael of Romania (represents British and American firms)
Sultan of Zanzibar (Seyyid Jamshid bin Abdullah keeps a little court in Portsmouth)
Idris of Libya (Cairo)
Constantine of Greece

Hostesses
IN
Davina Phillips
Homayoun Mazandi
Viscountess Rothermere
Lady Harlech
Marchioness of Bristol
Mrs. Peter Cadbury

FASHIONABLE	NOT SO FASHIONABLE
Bachelor hosts	
Andrew Ward-Jackson	Lord Weidenfeld
Sir Cecil Beaton	Lord Goodman
Norman St. John Stevas	
Simon Sainsbury (in the country)	
John Bowes-Lyon	

Millionaires	
IN	OUT
Sir Charles Forte	Alan Bristow
Lord Rothschild	Al Midani (owns the Dorchester and more besides)
Daniel K. Ludwig	
Lord Vestey	

Algy Cluff (of oil fame)	Sir James Goldsmith
Nigel Broackes (sic)	Sir David Brown
Christina Onassis	Sir James Hanson
N. Bunker Hunt	Arnold Weinstock
Giovanni Agnelli	Stavros Niarchos
Alain Chevasseur	Lord Kagan
Richard Northcott	Harry Hyams
Adnan Khashoggi	Robert de Balkany
Baron Heinrich Thyssen	
Paul Getty II	

Men about Town

IN	OUT
Lord (Charles) Greenock (an embryo playboy)	John Bentley
	Mark Shand
Marquess of Blandford (part time)	Jean Noel Grinda
	Gunther Sachs
Prince Ernst of Hanover	Mick Flick
Taki Theodoracopulos	Philip Martyn
Johnny Hesketh	Rupert Deen
Lord Burghersh	Constantine Niarchos
Dai Llewellyn (a few years yet in the old dog)	Nigel Pollitzer
Dodi Al Fayed	
Colin Tennant	
Sir William Pigott-Brown	

Models

IN	OUT
Marie Helvin	Barbara Dickson
Jerry Hall	Lauren Hutton
Clio Goldsmith	Veruschka
Cheryl Tiegs	Pauline Stone

Polly Eltes	Twigs (v. sixties now)
Amanda Bibby	Josephine Florent
Terry Markwell	Susan Harrison
Michel First	Hazel
Kim Harris	Mairi
Maudie James (making a comeback)	Valerie Catef
	Marianne Broome
Susie Dyson	Pattie Hanson
Rachel Ward	Kuni
Belinda Waite	Penelope Tree
Vanessa Downing	Linda Kerridge
Graham Rogers	
Colin Childs	
David Warbeck	
Alan Jones	
Lady Carina Fitzalan-Howard	

Gossip Columnists to cultivate
Nigel Dempster (becoming the doyen at a young age)
Lady Olga Maitland (kinder than most)
William Hickey
Stephen Lavers
Jack Martin (west coast USA)
Oliver Hush (for theatre talk)
Grovel/Colonel Mad (Private Eye)
Kenneth Rose (likes week-ending with subjects)

Photographers

IN	OUT
Lichfield	James Wedge
Steffano Massimo	Pat Booth
Barry Swabe	Norman Parkinson
Richard Young	Tom Hustler
Desmond O'Neill	

Snowdon
Derry Moore
David Bailey
Tony Boase
Helmut Newton
Duffy

Gina Lollabrigida
Don McCullin
Al Papparazzi
Terry Fincher

Other journalists

IN
Emma Soames
Tina Brown
Anna Raeburn
Lyndall Hobbs
Steffi Callan
Sandra Harris
Bea Miller
Ian Wooldridge
John Pilger
Peter Jenkins
Simon Jenkins
Auberon Waugh
Andrew Alexander
Fay Maschler

OUT
Jean Rook
Bel Mooney
Janet Street Porter
Alan Coren
Paul Callan
Bill Davis
Peter York
Chapman Pincher
Bernard Levin
Lord and Lady Vaizey
Patrick Hutber
Sid Yobo
Melvyn Bragg

Cartoonists

IN
Scarfe
Mac
Jak
Marc
Osbert Lancaster
Trog
Bill Tidy
Thelwell
Honeysett
ffolkes

OUT
Cummings
Giles
Barry Fantoni
Larry
Graham
Dickens
Mel Calman

MPs

IN	OUT
Ted Heath	Willie Whitelaw
Robert Adley	Nigel Lawson
David Alton (give him a chance)	Reginald Eyre
	Roy Hattersley
Nicholas Ridley	Enoch Powell
James Callaghan (of Middleton and Prestwich)	Clement Freud (should stick to food)
	Philip Whitehead
Kenneth Baker	Norman Lamont
Geoffrey Johnson Smith	Mrs. Sally Oppenheim
Willie Hamilton	Dr. David Owen (ex-public-schoolboy)
Michael Heseltine	
Eric Heffer (know thy enemy)	Leslie Huckfield
	Sir Timothy Kitson
Douglas Hurd	Winston Churchill
Hugh Fraser (a saintly man)	William Rees-Davies
Jonathan Aitken (smoothest man in the house)	

Ex-MPs

IN	OUT
Jeffrey Archer (now an author who claims popular success)	John Stonehouse
	Hugh Jenkins
	Helen Hayman
John Pardoe	Ernle Money
Brian Walden (the moderate TV interviewer)	Dick Taverne
	Maureen Colquhoun
Shirley Williams	
Teddy Taylor	

Interior Decorators

IN	OUT
Nicky Haslam	David Milnaric
Tessa Kennedy	Inchbald School students
Nina Campbell	Albrizzi
Charles Hammond	Neil Zarach
Jean Beaudrand	John Stefanides
Colefax and Fowler	Robin Anderson
Charlotte Clarke	
Christopher Vane Percy	
John Siddeley	

Thespians

IN	OUT
Jenny Agutter	Robert Powell
Judi Dench	Patrick Ryecart
Sinead Cusack	Simon Ward
Helen Mirren	All Redgraves except
Marsha Fitzalan-Howard	Vanessa
Diana Quick	Joan Collins
Vanessa Redgrave	Alexando Bastedo
Isabel Huppert	Joanna Lumley
Tom Courtenay	Prunella Gee
John Wood	Olivier Tobias
Roy Dotrice	Christopher Reeve
Lord Olivier	Susan George
Leonard Rossiter	Anthony Andrews
Sir John Gielgud	Arthur Mullard
Tom Conti	Vivienne Ventura
Sir Ralph Richardson	Edward Woodward
Janet Suzman	Patrick Mower
Sian Phillips	Gerald Harper
John Hurt	Michael Caine
Nigel Havers	Richard Johnson
Ian McShane	Tessa Dahl
Christopher Cazenove	Bianca Jagger (as an

Jenny Runacre	actress)
Maggie Smith	Jane Seymour
Gary Bond	Sylvia Kristel
Diana Rigg	Mynah Bird

some Polo types

IN	OUT
HRH Prince of Wales	Sinclair Hill
Lord Vestey	Lord Patrick Beresford
Sandy Harper	Guy Wildenstein
Major Ronnie Driver	Ginger Baker (of drum
Johnny Kidd	fame)
Lord Cowdray	Luis Sosa Basualdo
Julian Hipwood	Howard Hipwood
Eduardo Moore (but do not let him near your wife)	

some backgammon types

IN	OUT
Ian Hamilton (when able to find an opponent)	Paul Magriel
	Joe Dwek
	The Lorenz Brothers
	Philip Martyn
	Jean Noel Grinda
	Victor Lownes
	Lewis Deyong

Paid Persuaders

IN	OUT
Rodgers and Cowan (great party people — look for Margaret Gardner and Jeffrey Lane)	Galitzine and Partners
	John Addey (except for Bernard Thorold)
	Buckingham Palace Press Office (they are paid to

Theo Cowan
Liz Brewer
Tony Brainsby
Ingrid Seward
David Wynne-Morgan
Richard Laver
Nigel Neilson
Billy Hamilton

persuade you that it is
not true)
Gordon Reece
Serena Williams

Authors
IN
Edna O'Brien
Douglas Sutherland
Andrew Barrow
Carlos Castenada
Robin Maugham
Philip Roth
Kingsley Amis
Ian McEwan
William Burroughs
J. P. Donleavy
Anthony Burgess
  (Enderby period)
Jim Slater
Michael Frayn

Publishers
Jonathan Cape
Longmans
Allen & Unwin
Oxford University Press
Hamish Hamilton
Michael Joseph

(42)

Penguin
Macmillan
Heineman
Weidenfeld and Nicholson

Other members of the team

FASHIONABLE	ONCE FASHIONABLE
Davina Woodhouse	Michael Dupree
Sabrina Guinness	The Schumis
Billy Keating	James Mancham
Angela Gorgas	Emma de Vere Hunt
Kate Bush	Charlie Tennant
Lady Sophie Cavendish	Justin de Villeneuve
Lady Charlotte Greville	Zandra Rhodes
Michael White	Tommy Nutter
Leonard	David Shilling
Tina and Michael Chow	Oliver Musker
David Olivestone	Cathy McGowan
Anita Guinness	Christopher Hunter
Amschel Rothschild	John Aspinall
John Bowes-Lyon	Alex Scrimgeour
Michel Ermelin	Gervaise Williamson
Maria Niarchos	Jeremy Browne
Florence Grinda	Arabella Churchill
Lady Anne Lambton	Tim Hoare
Jonathan Bulmer	Bill Gibb
Kim Smith-Bingham	Christopher Cole
Benjie Mancroft	Michael Fish
Victoria Mancroft	Melissa Wyndham
Georgina Wynyard	Tom Gilby
Tara Tooth	Dr. Tony Greenburgh
Camilla Ferranti	David Iveson
Melody Wilson-	John Paul
Macdonald	Larry Adler
John Gold	Roy Miles

Peter Langan
Marguerite Littman
Peter Townend
Mark Birley
Andrew Fraser
Cosmo Fry
Lady Sarah Spencer
Rosamond Monckton
Daniel Topolski
Charles Delevinge
Ned Ryan
Charlotte Gordon-
  Cumming
Stash de Rollo
Bryan Ferry
Lucy Fox
Derek Jarman
George Melly
The Goldsmith sisters
Patricia Secunda
Tracy Chamoun
Piero de Monzi
Maxwell Aitken
Cosima Vane-Tempest-
  Stewart
Mark Slim
Manolo Blahnik
David Litchfield
Amanda Lear
Andrew Logan
Paula Yates
Benjy Clutterbuck
Bob Geldorff
Rupert Spicer
Philip Astor
Randle Siddeley

Bruce Oldfield
James Beard
Davina Sheffield
Jasper Conran
Michael Lindsay-Hogg
Christopher Monckton
John Rendall
Bruce Bossom
Sarah Forbes
Venetia Spicer
Quentin Crisp
Peter Moreton
Lynsey de Paul
Nicholas Egon
All toastmasters
Chantal d'Orthez
Steven Bentinck
Michael Pearson
Lady Antonia Fraser
Bianca Jagger
Margaret Trudeau
Jennifer Sharp
Roddy Llewellyn

Who to be seen lunching with
The Earl of Harewood at English National Opera House
Ava Gardner
The Duke of Norfolk in the Lords
Lord Olivier at National Theatre
Sir Michael Swan at the BBC canteen
Sir Charles Forte at Grosvenor House Hotel
James Hunt after a game of squash at the Marbella Club
Regine
Sir Iain Moncreiffe of that Ilk, at his club
Viscount Newport at the Caviar Bar
Prince Michael of Kent at Waltons
Margaret Thatcher at Flood Street or even better Scotney
    Castle
Sir John Rennie in his club
Earl of Lichfield at Scotts
Clio or Dido Goldsmith anywhere
Sir Clive Bossom at the RAC
Lady Tryon at Walton Street
Dai Llewellyn at Wedgies his new place of work
Anouschka Hempel at Blakes
Jasper Conran
Taki Theodoracopolous anywhere from Gstaad to
    Athens
Melody Wilson-Macdonald
Lady Falkender anywhere
Agapi Stassinopoulos
Mark Birley at Marks Club
Luis Sosa Basualdo
Ned Ryan
Lord Burghersh on your expense account
Lady Jane Wellesley at BBC canteen
Picnics with various members of the Royal Family at
    Badminton Horse Trials
Daniel K. Ludwig anywhere
Jenny Runacre

Addresses to have in London

IN	OUT
Some squares	
Belgrave (most exclusive of all)	Hyde Park
	Eaton (too noisy)
Grosvenor	Sussex
Hanover	Cavendish
Bryanston	Dorset
Chester	Argyll
Camden Hill	Berkeley (too commercial)
St. James's	Trevor
Edwardes	Gloucester
Dolphin	Powis
Finsbury (for city people)	Russell
Chelsea	Portman
Cadogan	

Other places	
Primrose Hill	Bayswater
Fulham Road	King's Road
Prince of Wales Drive, Battersea	Park Lane (not U at all)
	Hackney (trendy lefties)
Brook Green (for the not so rich)	Cromwell Road
	Limehouse
Hans Place	Earl's Court (don't even drive along it)
Thornhill Crescent (getting smarter)	
	Marble Arch
St. Katharine's Dock	Putney
Royal Avenue	Portabello
Kensington Palace Gardens	Soho
Wilton Crescent	
The Boltons	

Which county?

IN	OUT
West Sussex	East Sussex

Suffolk	Kent
North Yorkshire	West and South Yorkshire
Dorset	Devon
Hereford	Hertfordshire
Shropshire	Buckinghamshire
Perthshire	Lancashire
Peebleshire	Derbyshire
Argyllshire	Essex
Wiltshire	Roxburghshire
Somerset	Norfolk
Northamptonshire	Cleveland
Gloucestershire	Lincolnshire
Cumbria	Merseyside
Oxfordshire	Cambridgeshire

6

The Country Weekend

INVITATIONS to certain country houses must be sought because although it is no longer unfashionable to be spotted walking the streets of the capital between Friday night and Monday morning, much fun can be had in the shires.

If many house parties are not as formal as they were, due to lack of staff, more than a few families still observe the strict rules of etiquette. It is a crime to be late for meals, otherwise cook gets in a terrible flap and threatens resignation. This will make you most unpopular with the hostess — who cannot boil an egg. If one is ever envious of the owner of stately houses it is a comfort to realise that they nearly always lead a regimented life to avoid up-setting the staff.

An insufficient tip to the butler or footman (some still exist) and your car will be the only one belonging to the guests which is still dirty when, much to your chagrin, it is delivered to the front on your departure.

Faux pas are easily made in the forty-eight hours that you are a guest (or prisoner) in a strange environment where you have to think of others. Thus the hot bath full up to the plughole is not encouraged.

Disaster could set in when the first-time visitor dutifully unpacks his own case when there is a maid to do that task. Immediately you will be exposed, to the watchful staff at least, who will realise that you are not quite what you seem. They will regard and treat you as one of themselves and call you 'love'. Everything they do for you will be done a little grudgingly and only a generous (not too generous) tip will win back some of their esteem.

(49)

. . . dutifully unpacks his own case.

Tales of horror are told about house parties which, even if apocryphal, serve as a warning that hidden pitfalls lie before the unwary guest.

One friend of mine enjoyed a night with the host's daughter, who, because she knew the way about the house at three in the morning without treading on squeaky floorboards and waking the dogs, arranged to come to his bedroom.

Their illicit meeting remained undetected until the next morning when the Spanish maid was turning down the guest's bed to find his sheets streaked with vivid orange stains and reported her curious find to the hostess.

Having summoned her daughter she discovered after interrogation the goings-on of the previous night. Careless Emma had been using tanning lotion on her legs much of which had come off on her boyfriend's bedding. When challenged he could offer no defence and was despatched from the house forthwith.

Another man put up a terrible black by sitting rather clumsily on the sofa and on the family Chihuahua — killing the pet instantly. There is no way out of that one.

Then there was the time when having retired to bed full of wine and port, the first-time visitor awoke several hours before breakfast desperate to use the lavatory.

After a fruitless search around the darkened corridors (including a mistaken entry into the hostess's bedroom) he returned to his own room — there to find salvation in the form of a commode. Morning arrived and with it the problem of disposal.

With the house buzzing with life the guest decided a trip to the lavatory was an impossible task, so he decided to throw the contents of the chamber pot out of the window.

Naturally the handle detached itself from the pot and in compliance with Newton's law it hurtled down through

. . . illicit meetings.

the conservatory window—leaving the guest with a difficult explanation to make at breakfast.

Hosts vary in their generosity from those who put everything they own at the disposal of their guests to those who order the butler to switch the electricity off at the mains at 10.30, and thus force everyone to bed.

At one Scottish house party so meagre was the hospitality that it ended with the guests seeking revenge on their mean host and even meaner butler by burying most of the family silver in the garden—where one day some treasure hunter will probably alight upon it.

Houses to head for

Chatsworth
Blenheim
Scotney Castle (Mrs. Thatcher's country flat)
Truncheons
Llanfair Grange
Sherston
Harewood House
Weston Park
Bolton Castle
Sandringham
Eaton Hall
Wilton House
Stowell Park
Woburn Abbey (when closed to the public)
Longleat (as above)
Floors Castle
Highclere
Stratfield Saye
Charlton Park

7

Appearance

SARTORIAL elegance seems to be making a comeback for both sexes—especially those who attend an office. Radical chic, as documented by Tom Wolfe, is dead. Bells, beads, gypsy frocks, patchwork jeans, Chelsea boots (remember?), long hair and beards belong to a generation past. In its place has arrived a type of shabby smartness which needs money and care to create the right effect.

Army colours, which were so despised in the Nixonian days, are now IN. Khaki fatigues (perhaps a final statement about Vietnam) are heavily in evidence at the smartest dinner party, the fashionable wedding and the progressive office.

Leather has made a spectacular comeback, collars have shrunk in size so much that pencil thin ties are the only ones which do not look out of proportion. The flared trouser has been forgotten and lapels have gone the way of collars.

But really fashion has lost its way and now exists largely to keep the designers and manufacturers in pocket and their followers out of it. Unlike in America where they slavishly follow each other (Annie Hall, Farrah Fawcett Majors), such is their insecurity, the more independent British female is dressing more or less as she wants.

Thanks to the Punks nothing is too outrageous, and young stockbrokers hang-up their suits at home and hit the town in tight leathers and a discreet earring. Everything from boiler-suits to creations by Yuki and Chloe is acceptable at dinner parties.

The ubiquitous pin-stripe (the unfortunate Earl of

Gypsy OUT — elegance IN

Lucan had nothing else) will not lie down and die. As Nigel Dempster, a conventional if snappy dresser, has said, it has never been unfashionable to buy clothes from certain designers like St. Laurent — provided they are worn with abandon not timidity.

As in every social avenue it is a crime to be seen to be trying. Beware of labels men — the person who wears the Gucci shoes with the biggest buckle and his trousers just a fraction too short, rather like members of the Leander rowing club are prone to do.

Watch out for the wearer with the tie that has the maker's emblem emblazoned all over it, or the suit which has one too many labels advertising both the dresser's bad taste and the name of his Savile Row tailor.

It is sagacious to regard with suspicion the slightly too well dressed man because, like the owner of a new Rolls Royce, there is scant chance of his being a gentleman.

Similarly, the woman with too generous an application of Joy, although it is the most expensive perfume in the world and is used by the Queen, is trying to make a statement. To advertise the fact that you are rich in so blatant a manner can only lead to disaster.

In no other country is it easier to place a person in their respective socio-economic division by just looking at them . . . so in matters of dress the social interloper must tread with care.

Accessories

IN	OUT
Signet rings (must be worn on the little finger of the left hand and for women on the little finger of the right hand)	Wedding rings for men
	Bogus signet rings (do not be fooled)
	Digital watches
	Diamond cufflinks or ones made from coins etc.

Watch out for the wearer whose suit has one too
many labels . . .

Cartier watches

Cufflinks in either silver or gold but without family crests

Tab collars (making a comeback)

Smoking jackets

Money-clips

Collar pins

Tie pins (very non-U)

Make-love-not-war type buttons

All shoes for men with gold buckles

Two-tone (co-respondents) shoes

Shoes with built-up heels except cowboy boots

Bowler hats (except for stewards at Royal Ascot and shipyard managers)

Money purses for men

Fob watches (pompous)

Waistcoats

Handkerchiefs which match shirts

Neckerchiefs

Garters for men

Fake pearls

False eyelashes

Headscarves in town (S.L. wear)

Huskey jackets

Women's shoes

IN	OUT
Manolo Blahnik	Gucci
Kurt Geiger	Rayne
Bruno Magli	Elliot
Midas	K Shoes
Zapata	Russell and Bromley
Terry de Havilland	Ravel
Charles Jourdan	
Guido Pasquali	

Men's shoes

IN	OUT
Bally	Harrods
Lobb's (for snobs)	Gucci
Wildsmith	Russell and Bromley
Foster	Poulsen, Skone and Co.
Tricker's	

Shirtmakers

IN	OUT
Turnbull and Asser	Hilditch & Key
Deborah and Clare (main rivals to T&A)	Jermyn Street Shirtmakers
Harvie & Hudson	Coles
James Drew	Hong Kong/Empire made

Top Designers

Jean Muir
Lanvin
Bruce Oldfield
Yuki
Dior
Belville Sassoon
Hardy Amies
St. Laurent
Adrian Cartmell
Etienne Aigner
Jousse (Sportif)
Courrèges
Thea Porter
Bill Gibb

Jewellers

IN	OUT
Tessiers	Garrards
Aspreys	Algernon Asprey

Gerard
Kutchinsky
Boucheren
Piaget
Philip Antrobus
Cartier, London

Mappin and Webb
Graff
Andrew Grima
Torrini
Ratners

Perfumes

IN	NOT SO IN
Joy by Patou	Vu by Ted Lapidus
Chanel No: 19	Chanel No: 5
Cavale	Femme by Rochas
Givenchy	Blue Grass
Guerlain	Blase
Paco Rabanne	Opium
Lagerfield	Charlie
Azzaro	
Courrèges	
Arpège	
Alliage	

Tailors

IN	OUT
Hawes and Curtis	Gieves and Hawkes Ltd.
Johns and Pegg (a little conservative)	Harrods
	Zographon (Carnaby St.)
Kilgour, French and Stanbury	Henry Poole
Vincent	Anderson and Sheppard
Blades	Nutters
H. Huntsmen and Sons	

Hair Cutters

IN	OUT
Leonard	Scissors
Gavin Hodge	Vidal Sassoon

Molton Brown
Schumi, Pont Street
The Salon Lobetta
Michael John
Mane Line
Harambee
Joseph Kendall

Toni and Guy
Harrods barber shop
Ricci Burns
Stafford and Frieda
Oro
Little Maurice

Furs—where to buy them
Zwirn
Harrods
National Fur Company
Norman Furs
Maxwell Croft
Frank Cooney
Calman Links
Bonham's sales
Witte
Femina Paul

Health Farms

Society reveres, and has always revered, beautiful women and men. Unlike in the East where fatness is a visible means of judging a man's prosperity, slimness is IN. This is heartening news for the owners of health farms—a booming business in beleaguered Britain. Visiting these establishments when the ravages of too many parties, a surfeit of champagne and late nights have done nothing for the complexion or waistline is most fashionable. Forking out £100 a day to live under an enforced regime of lettuce leaves, carrot juice, lemon tea and early-to-bed discipline may seem a ridiculous way for intelligent life to carry on.

Vanity is important. The true child of society knows that it is his/her duty to look after the body. True, geniuses and opera singers may be fat, but they have

. . . £100 a day for a lettuce leaf.

other talents to offer and the general rule is that beer guts (and their kin) are strictly for people who will not be reading this book.

A few days in purdah at a health farm (some would say it is the ultimate absurdity when half the world has trouble feeding itself) at least calms troubled minds, trims bodies and wallets and gives the visitor a feeling of immense triumph having kicked haute cuisine, the cocktail circuit and the rat race — for two weeks at least.

Health Farms
Stobo Castle
Forestmere
Eaton Hall
Grayshott Hall
Henlow Grange
Inglewood
Shrublands
Shenley Lodge
Champneys

8

Where introductions are made

LONDON lacks the chic of Paris and the brash extrovert atmosphere of New York, and this is reflected in the night-club scene. There is not one niterie in the capital which could accurately be described as 'exclusive' — a much overworked word.

The English do not on the whole like to mix with one another (unless a war or national disaster forces them to), while the Italians and Americans can more easily find something in common with one another. New York's Studio 54, which at times was the scene of spontaneous shows of orgiastic decadence, would I suspect not work this side of the big pond.

The British do not like to make fools of themselves — which is why they are the worst dancers on earth — and have a fear of removing their clothing in public. They do, however, have a capacity for enjoyment, which is why a spate of clubs opened their doors for business in the dying moments of the Labour Government.

Society remains as fickle as the April weather and transfers its allegiance from one establishment to another before the ranks not on the inside can realise it. This enables the members of the First Division to be courted by club owners and to accept their hospitality in return for their patronage which the hopeful proprietor thinks will attract paying guests. It is a system which works. Thus anybody who thinks he is somebody will have a wallet full of honorary membership cards.

Any climber worth his salt will be a frequent visitor to the more acceptable clubs and express ignorance of the ones which have fallen out of favour.

Just as the New York crowd deserted Studio 54 for the more heterosexual atmosphere of Xenon, their London counterparts have turned away from places like Wedgie's and Bennett in Battersea and gone for the more racy spots such as the Embassy and Maunkberry's.

I present a personal guide to the night scene, which because of its above mentioned fickle nature, could have changed by the time you read this. But if you are in the know you WILL know where to find the *cognoscenti*.

Night Clubs

IN	OUT
Annabel's (the only place in London where Prince Charles can be spotted bopping and where gossip columnists are banned. Dark enough for naughty behaviour)	Regine's (not a patch on her Parisian club—high prices have attracted a Middle Eastern clientele and Bianca Jagger)
Tramp (denizens include footballers, pop-singers, swingers. Not as lively as it once was)	Bennett (this Battersea non-event with a Roddy Llewellyn garden had just two days of glory and attracts out of school upstarts)
Maunkberry's (just along from Tramp in Jermyn Street and frequented by a gay element, media and rock stars)	Wedgie's (the set that attracted all the publicity when it opened have vanished because, says Lord Burghersh, the former resident host, they cannot afford the prices)
Embassy (not the chic place it once was with heavy gay element and can be as smelly as Venice in the Summer)	J. Arthurs (post-punk and rather second division members)
The Global Village roller-disco (enjoying some	Dial 9 (too tame and is

popularity but how long will this imported fad last?)

redolent of a private sitting room)

Le Privé (expensive but not where it is at)

Valbonne (Rugby parties from St. Helen's might like this display of phantasmagoria)

Raffles (they insist on the wearing of jacket and tie. This attracts a staid following who must enjoy dancing in a library — which it resembles)

Morton's (a shadow of its former self)

Scheherazade (not in the ranks of the fashionable)

Gentlemen's clubs

The existence of such quaint institutions as the gentleman's club might seem an anachronism in these days of Ceefax, Concorde and sex equality, but a cluster of them exist around St. James's to serve the needs of an entrenched few — whose greatest fear is the invasion of women into their hallowed inner sanctums.

If no nightclub in London can be described as 'exclusive', there exists among the remaining ranks of the gentleman's clubs one which Groucho Marx (who didn't care to be a member of an organisation which would have him as a member) would never have been invited to join. Both his profession and ethical background were wrong. It is White's.

. . . the only private Turkish Bath which allows
journalists.

The membership roll reads like a list of the peerage, and it can only be regarded as a social triumph to become a member — if only to make use of the splendidly stocked tent during Royal Ascot.

Other more realistic clubs, like the once-sumptious RAC which possesses the only private Turkish Bath in London, a gym, four squash courts and a Romanesque pool which would please Cleopatra, have had to bow to modern trends.

Economics took over, women were invited to use the facilities and the membership was opened up to shop owners, book-keepers and journalists.

While not an essential card in the climber's hand, membership to a well-chosen club will at least provide a useful meeting place full of the people who either run, or know people who run, the country. This is an invaluable asset for the commercially inclined.

The disadvantages of membership will mean tolerating (in most cases) the type of food that is served up at Public School, The Inns of Court and the House of Lords.

IN	OUT
White's	East India, Sports, Public
Beefsteak	Schools and Devonshire
Athenaeum	Oxford and Cambridge
Boodle's	Royal Automobile
Brooks's	Eccentric
Savile	Carlton
Garrick	
Pratt's	

Gaming clubs

PLACES WHERE TO LOSE THE ESTATE	PLACES WHERE NOT TO LOSE THE ESTATE
Aspinall's	Curzon House
Clermont	Playboy

Crockford's

Le Cercle at Les
Ambassadeurs

Victoria Sporting Club

Hertford

Palm Beach

Ladbroke

Knightsbridge

Connoisseur

9

Sex, Manners and Marriage

MAYBE manners no longer maketh man but in the tricky areas of sexual behaviour there are general rules to obey or be broken. It has always seemed unjust that a promiscuous girl quickly begets a reputation as a whore, while her randy male counterpart is fondly referred to as a stud or lady-killer. It is not quite as clear-cut as that, because in some circles the Lothario can gain a reputation which will work against him—applauded by members of his own sex but regarded with suspicion by the fair victims on which he preys. To be branded a seducer and worse still to be known as a sexual braggart might do wonders for the ego, but such a reputation is not something to have hanging around one's neck when the real thing (an heiress) presents itself. "I know this man's reputation—what are his motives,"—"What is he after—my body, my money or my soul?"

Affairs, be they in marriage or out of it, between the older woman and the younger man or between members of the same sex, should be conducted with discretion. Society is a bitchy place. Because no gentleman ever talks about his conquests the chances of the liaison reaching too many ears will be minimised. This is essential for relationships which are as quickly over as the asparagus season.

The flirt, that is not to say the female teaser who is liable to land herself in trouble, is held in esteem because, like a Red Admiral flitting from flower to flower, he dusts people with a *joie de vivre*. He might be a wolf in sheep's clothing as he sprinkles his charm about, but he never lets his intentions be known.

. . . more important flatters their mothers.

His approach is all lightness, mystery and sophistication as he flatters young girls and, more important, their mothers who will be affected by his attention. He will employ the social kiss both to the face and when the occasion is right to the hand.

Marriage between pubescent partners is not to be encouraged and is out of fashion—although there are exceptions to the rule. Most couples experience living together, which no longer shocks parents, and the greater permissiveness has made obsolete the phrase 'living in sin'.

Asking fathers for the hand of their daughters might seem an anachronism today but the habit goes on. It is a harmless act which, if one's prospective spouse comes from a moneyed background, can only be prudent and politic.

There is nothing so tedious as newly marrieds with their stolen glances at each other over dinner tables, but cohabitation has helped erode that early flush of self-satisfaction.

One of the most successful pressure groups of the 1970s has been Gay Lib whose progress has far outstripped what the earlier movement, Women's Lib, tried to do for their sex. I never did think hairy female legs were an attractive proposition.

Apart from robbing the English language of a useful three letter word the Gay Libbers have given their followers self-respect and a voice in society which amounts to a cult.

Whereas in the past it was a bonus to be homosexual in artistic and culinary fields, it is now acceptable in many diverse areas with the probable exceptions of politics and the civil and diplomatic services.

Clubs whose appeal is specific to the homosexual (which is not to say heterosexuals do not attend them) have sprung up and owners have made no secret of the fact, dressing waiters in satin shorts, a smile, and little else.

If society now regards the homosexual male as a refreshing tonic to "straights" — black became beautiful in the 60's — the lesbian has not received the same approbation. Perhaps their turn will come in the next decade.

DO'S	DONT'S
Flirt	Brag about sexual conquests
Ask for Lucy's hand in marriage	Discuss sexual performance
Get up when someone walks into the room (for males)	Go to wife swapping parties as they are a product of suburban living
Wait to start your meal until the hostess begins hers	Call homosexuals "irons" or nancy boys
Walk on the inside of a woman in a street until coaches make a comeback	Pet/neck in a restaurant as it is boring for others
Open car doors for women when getting in — not necessary when disembarking	Marry before 29 (men) or 24 (women)
Swear in mixed company — many blue bloods use blue language	Give up seats on a bus or train to someone not in need of one
Elope because it is a romantic notion, but not to Gretna Green	Go to sex shops
Compliment someone on hair, dress, food, house, etc.	Be late for dinner parties
	Ignore people you have met before when you come across them
	Forget to reciprocate hospitality
	Have family rows in front of other people

Don't be late for dinner parties

Reply to invitations

Be effusive when Jeremy gives you an evening at the opera, but do not insist he comes in for coffee if you want to sleep alone

Announce your marriage in The Times (here's hoping) or The Daily Telegraph

Interrupt a partner in the middle of telling a story

Drop names of people you have never met or you will be found out

Leave a dining table in the middle of a meal unless it is a matter of life or death

Where to be married and by whom

IN	OUT
St. Peter's, Eaton Square	Houses of Parliament crypt
St. Bride's, Fleet Street	Guards' Chapel
Westminster Abbey (for Royals)	Chelsea register office
Brompton Oratory	Paddington register office
At any country church	Las Vegas
By your favourite ship's captain	On American TV (Tiny Tim)
	St. Clement Danes, Strand

Places for receptions

IN	OUT
30, Pavilion Road	Tramp
Claridges	Dorchester
Savoy River Room	Inn on the Park
Les Ambassadeurs	The Hilton
The Institute of Directors, Pall Mall	RAC Country Club, Epsom
St. James's Palace (not exactly open for hire but there are ways)	Grosvenor House Hotel

Orangery, Holland Park
A marquee in your garden/
  estate in the country

Love Tokens

Him to her

IN	OUT
A ball in her honour	A dozen red roses
12oz bottle of Joy or her favourite perfume	A Cartier watch
Flying lessons	A year's subscription to The Tatler
An account at Hoare's started off with £1,000	Her weight in gems (a foreign custom)
A portrait by Edward Halliday	A fortnight at Champneys (this gesture might be taken the wrong way)
An American Express card	A mini bar of gold (non-U)
A week at Michel Guérard's restaurant-spa in the South of France	A heart made of ebony
An emerald	Membership to Regines
A single pearl in an oyster shell	A Magimix (not for lovers)
A Concorde ticket to Rio (return)	Earrings in lapis-lazuli
A pair of peach-faced love-birds	A set of luggage
A love nest on the Italian lakes	A caged canary
A book of poems by e. e. cummings	A ring with your family crest on it
A season ticket to Covent Garden	A course at a cookery school
A Piaget watch	The complete works of Shakespeare
A Hermes scarf	A season ticket to National Trust homes and gardens

A dozen red roses and a caged canary . . .

Her to him

IN	OUT
The key to her flat	An antique telephone
A hunter/racehorse	Tickets for a QE2 cruise
A Chippendale chair	An eternity ring
A jar of truffles	A year's subscription to The Field
A case of Château d'Yquem	One red rose (cliché)
A 1lb pot of Sevruga from USSR	Aftershave
A hand made silk shirt from one of the IN makers (see list)	A subscription to the MCC
A white silk opera scarf	A dog (he may not want it)
A Cartier money clip in gold	A cigarette lighter (not original)
A subscription to Wentworth Golf Club (or other course)	Fleece lined gloves
Fishing rights on the Tweed for a season	A manicure set
A pair of Purdeys (for the rich)	A pewter tankard
A video tape recorder and camera	A monogrammed glass
A snuff box	Slippers and socks
A meal out at his favourite restaurant	The complete works of Dickens
A Kadinski print	Coffee mugs with his name on them
A dressing gown to match hers	

10

Restaurants

THESE remain a dangerous area for social inter-
lopers—for a chance remark to a waiter can reveal much
about the status of an individual.

It is not good form to send back dishes to the kitchen
unless one is able to detect that the chef has left the
orange juice out of the crêpes suzette or there is a slug in
the salad.

It is a show-off who allows the wine waiter to give him a
chance to test a carafe plonk or declares a bottle corked—
a very rare occurence. Certainly sniff, sip and savour a
Lynch Bages but wave on the Soave after ensuring it is
well chilled. As a guest the socially insecure might address
his orders directly to a host ignoring a hovering waiter
which is sheer pomposity. And then there is another pit-
fall—what to choose to eat.

Avoid garlic dishes if the rest of the evening is to be
spent in company. Do not display your gastronomic
ignorance by ordering prawn cocktail—this disaster can
turn up disguised in Italian or French menu language.
Tournedos Rossini more often than not turns out to be
a piece of meat deposited on top of a wedge of cheap
(probably tinned) paté and a doorstep of fried bread. It
does nothing for the figure or for enhancing a feeling of
well-being.

A knowledge of restaurateurs and cooking methods is
not pretentious and can only add to your charm. Know
about Bourdin at the Connaught Hotel Restaurant as
well as what Bocuse is doing in France.

Pre-prandial drinks, if you regard yourself as a
gourmet, should not be spirits but either a fortified wine

A show off who tests the carafe plonk . . .

like sherry, Campari or any aperitif. Because the British have a low reputation as gourmets this rule is often broken by quite discerning people.

Since smoking has gone out of fashion it is still not considered polite to do so between courses.

The most likely person to break the rules of gastronomy will probably be a well-established member of the club. He is frequently the person who can tell blue jokes in mixed company, eat well-done steaks and break wind without giving offence. It is best not to try these ploys.

Restaurant Guide

IN	OUT
L'Escapade	Jules Bar
San Lorenzo (beautiful people)	Langan's Brasserie
	Lockets
Cecconi's	Lacy's
Ma Cuisine	Friends
Waltons	Mirabelle
Connaught Hotel Restaurant	Le Gavroche
	Grosvenor House, La Fontaine
Wiltons	
Gay Hussar	Savoy Grill
Savoy Restaurant	Rules
Kalamaras Taverna	San Frediano
White Tower	Dorchester Grill and Terrace Restaurant
Golden Duck	
Poons (Lisle Street)	Poons, Covent Garden
Fingles	Bistro Vinos (all)
Scott's	Asterix
Parkes	Joe Allens
Tandoori of Mayfair	Kundan
Le Suquet	Claridge's Restaurant
Thomas de Quincey	Shezan
Wild Thyme	Leith's

The most unlikely people smoke between courses.

Holy Cow	Lee Ho Fook (all)
Khan's	Kettner's
Chez Moi	Simpson's in the Strand
Odins	I Paparazzi
Paper Tiger	Overton-St. James's
Inn on the Park, Four Seasons	Ivy
	Lafayette
Hard Rock (for youth)	Pooh Corner

Out of Town

IN	OUT
Box Tree, Ilkley	Elizabeth, Oxford
Horn of Plenty, Gulworthy	Hole-in-the-Wall, Bath
	Alfonso's, Suffolk
Thornbury Castle, Avon	Pool Court, Pool-in-Wharfedale
Hintlesham Hall, Suffolk	
Southampton General	Hungry Monk, Jevington
Heatherwood Hospital, Ascot	Lodore Swiss Hotel, Restaurant, Keswick
Chez Nico, Dulwich	Skindles, Maidenhead
McCoy's, Straddle Bridge	Kildwick Hall, Yorkshire
Sharrow Bay, Ullswater	
Chewton Glen Hotel, Marryat Room	
Woodstock, Bear Hotel	
Complete Angler Hotel, Valaisan Restaurant, Marlow	

LEAGUE DIVISION ONE HOTELS	LEAGUE DIVISION TWO HOTELS
Connaught (for Chef Bourdin's food)	Hotel Bristol
	Portman
Capital	Churchill

Inn on the Park
Blake's
Portobello
Brown's
Claridge's
Carlton Tower
Stafford
Savoy (just)
Howard
Ritz (still best for tea)
Berkeley
Inter-Continental

Hilton (both)
Park Tower
Hyde Park
Dorchester
Grosvenor House
Waldorf
Cumberland
Strand Palace
Athenaeum
Selfridge
Londonderry
Royal Lancaster
Duke's
Cunard International
Holiday Inn (Chelsea)

11

Drinking

THE social mountaineer would not dare fob his guests off with "a fruity little and reasonably priced Orvieto", but he could get away with and impress with a new Californian discovery or a Rioja from Spain. There is a danger that the over eager will produce vast quantities of Dom Perignon, Roederer Cristal or Tattinger's fine Comtes de Champagne and be exposed as climbers—although their guests will accept their lavish hospitality with alacrity.

Champagne is a drink central to society—and many members will try to obtain as much of it as they possibly can for free. Art gallery and night-club openings are good in this respect, followed closely by sponging off those characters who are attempting to join the set.

Cheap champagne is easily detected by large bubbles, so it is no good having the hired butler swathe the bottle in a napkin. Sparkling wine is equally unacceptable unless it is to go into a mixture like Black Velvet (out).

The serving of over-extravagant wines before a meal could similarly expose an intruder. But a dinner party is one occasion where a Grand Cru Chablis could be produced, or a '66 Latour Haut Brion, without seeming too showy and suspicion would not be caused.

Do not pass the wine test and get the shape of the glass wrong like Americans so often do. Use a flute for champagne but never a saucer type glass which is for Babycham—what ever that may be.

The tulip, which is also fine for champagne, can be used for Clarets and the larger Paris goblet for more robust Burgundy wines. Monster balloon glasses are never

Cheap champagne is detected by big bubbles.

used by experts for cognac and people who have brandy
warming equipment should not be reading this book.

Drinks

IN	OUT
Campari and soda/tonic	Dubonnet
Dry Martini (U.S. style)	Gin and Orange
Bloody Mary	Lager and Lime
Vodka/Polish Spirit for men	Bourbon and Canadian Whisky
Tequila Sunrise	Real Ale (it has produced the beer bore)
Malt Whisky (strictly no ice)	Sweet sherry
German Ale	Italian wine (most)
Californian wine (most)	'Throwing' Champagne
French wine (most except South F)	Mead
	Irish Mist
Harvey Wallbangers	Brandy Alexander
Kirsch	Southern Comfort
Creme de Menthe frappé	Black Velvet
Scrumpy	Ouzo (who has not been to Greece?)
Perrier Water	
Tap Water (very chic to ask for this)	Absinthe
	Schnapps
Arrack (foul but shows you have travelled)	Sangria
	Chasers
Calvados	Sake
Planter's Punch	
Fernet Branca (for the day after)	
Port	
Cointreau	

Drinking places

IN	OUT
Trader Vics	Post Office Tower

Les Ambassadeurs
Jules Bar
Fortnum's Spanish Bar
Zanzibar
Edens
VIP lounge Heathrow
Your favourite week-end
  pub in the country
Julies
At home

El Vino
Wine Bars
London pubs (except The
  Grenadier)
The Harrod's Pub
Moretons, Berkeley
  Square
21 Club
White Elephant
Departmental Stores
Curzon House

12

Sport

THE reason why parents send their children to public school is because they regard it as a fine investment which will, like a well-chosen share, show profitable returns later. Prospective parents are always rushed by the headmaster through badly heated classrooms, dingy dining rooms, sordid dormitories and out onto the playing fields.

Here the master with an expansive gesture ends the tour and as the parents tread the sward he says: "You know, Mrs. Fothergill, here we have 10 grass tennis courts, four squash courts, a firing range and sixty acres of pitches and, oh yes, the boys can take riding lessons."

Immediately the parents are won over, because even if battles were not won on the playing fields of Eton friendships certainly were. It is these associations, not academic honours, the ambitious parent realises, that will stand their kin in good stead later on.

As it happens, to be 'sportif' is highly fashionable as people are once again taking care of their bodies, which, if they are serious socialites will take a hard pounding during the course of duty.

The p.s. boy may have hated sport at school and rebelled every afternoon when at five below he was quite properly expected to turn out for Rugby. It is a mistake to eschew sport upon leaving as it is disastrous when, for instance, you are invited to play tennis and you don't even know the rudimentary elements of the game.

Cricket produces bores (Harold Pinter) but it is undoubtedly THE English game, although colonists like the Australian and West Indian get the emphasis wrong by trying to win at any cost. Every socialite has his G & M or

Women should not play cricket . . .

SS, a pair of boots with nails coming up inside and sweater and cap with school colours. These garments can be plucked from the cupboard when one is asked to play a charity or beer match and no shame is incurred because of a faint smell of mothballs.

Women, on the other hand, should not play cricket — those that have are usually spotted a mile off because, I think, it is something to do with the way they sit. Lacrosse, although not a bit ladylike, is somehow more acceptable.

Football, although originally promoted by public schools, is now beyond the pale. It is no longer a game which can be socially useful and the only way is to express complete ignorance of it until the World Cup comes around — there is no way of avoiding that competition.

Golf, too, has lost its exclusivity although its introduction to lorry drivers and shopkeepers has done nothing to produce any British world class competitors.

For pure social climbing shooting remains the best sport to adopt, but it is also among the most expensive and because the etiquette is designed to keep human beings alive and game dead it is a tortuous world for the upstart.

In order to follow the social calendar it is important to have more than a cursory interest in the world of the horse — although confessing a complete ignorance of things equine is no longer considered to be social death by fair-minded moderns. An ability to sit in the saddle and not look as if you are about to fall off is an advantage and also it helps to know something of racing so as not to have a miserable time at Ascot . . . although to many that event is lunch in the White's tent and a vast alfresco cocktail party.

Sailing is no longer the sport of Kings and it is a diversion which attracts more *nouveau riche* than almost any other field. This is not to say no interest should be shown

Continentals apt to laugh at our efforts on the slopes.

towards boats—some glamorous parties are held aboard yachts, notably at Monte Carlo during Grand Prix week and Cannes during the rather awful film festival.

Winter sports are the social climber's dream when the Concorde-set are gathered together in one place to give expression to their sybaritic urges. Although invented by the British, we show little aptitude for winter sports and continentals are apt to laugh at our efforts on the slopes.

For the purposes of this book the social athlete need not be a Jean Claude Killy but he/she has to look right and head for the right resorts (see Winter holidays) whose *aprés ski* centre is Gstaad. It is well known that the serious skier who has been out on the slopes all day will have no energy for what must be considered to be the important time—after dark. The skiing around Gstaad is by no means the finest to be offered in the Alps, but it has the best nightlife and The Palace Hotel is never without the odd guest famous enough to settle the bill by signing the table cloth.

IN	OUT
Jogging (it is fashionable to wear the track-suit almost anywhere)	Athletics
	Association football
	Surfing
Sail-surfing	Knur and spell (a game for Yorkshiremen, not gentlemen)
Hunting	
Shooting	
Fishing	Boxing
Cricket	Badminton
Hockey	Table tennis
Rugby football	Volleyball (an American import)
Snooker	
Winter sports	Rugby league (a game for miners)
Golf	
Yoga	Billiards
Rugby Fives	Water sports

The over-and-under and the unruly dog . . .

Sailing (for Cowes etc.)	Judo
Squash	Cycling
Tennis	Eton fives
Real tennis	The Wall Game (Eton)
Polo	Shove ha'penny
Hang-gliding	Darts
Gliding	Skittles
Lacrosse	Mountaineering
Hurling (for Scotsmen)	Sky-diving
	Frisbee
	Pot-holing

Shooting

One of the best ways to social climb is to be invited onto one of the better grouse moors or pheasant shoots. But because Germans, Americans, Greeks and Arabs are willing to pay up to £400 a day to desport themselves on our unique moors, and many owners are quick to exploit the commercial prospects, invitations are hard to come by.

The problems start when the guest, having boasted sufficiently about his markmanship, is invited to spend a couple of days' shooting. From now on he is constantly on trial. He must live up to his claim and not miss every other bird which flies over him. He must bring with him the right type of gun and his dog must be as well-behaved as its owner, who has the added concern of dressing correctly. A yapping dog and one that does not obey its owner's commands is liable to end up accidently shot. Terrible blacks can be put up against the man who continually 'poaches' birds which were rightly destined for the neighbouring gun, and to shoot at a hen pheasant on a cocks-only day is tantamount to social suicide.

To use an over and under shotgun for anything other than clay pigeon or skeet shooting is not done because it is considered unsporting and ungentlemanly — and all further promises of shooting will fail to materialise. But

(97)

to use a cheap Spanish-made gun is quite acceptable, while a matching set of Purdey guns, which these days cost many thousands, is considered to be an investment.

The emphasis of the organised shoot has changed since Edwardian times when the Prince of Wales, who was too fat to hut, made the sport popular. Those wishing to curry favour with Royalty immediately stocked their estates with masses of game and extended an invitation to HRH. The days of such vast slaughter are now over and almost everyone (and the Game Conservancy) regard record bags to be a vulgar anachronism.

Guns

IN	OUT
Purdey	Webley and Scott
Churchill	Cogswell and Harrison
H. Atkin	J. Woodward
Army and Navy	C. Lancaster
Holland and Holland	
William Evans	
Spanish (various)	

Estates

IN	OUT
Bolton Abbey, Duke of Devonshire	Althorp, Earl Spencer (gone too commercial)
Roxby, Lord Tranmire	The Trefford estate in East Anglia (the bags are too big to be in)
Harewood, The Earl of Harewood	
Six Mile Bottom (best partridge shoot in the West)	Sandringham (mainly wild birds who do not fly well anyway)
Drumlanrig Castle Dumfries-shire, Duke of Buccleuch	Charles Forte's Irish shoot
	Arkengarthdale, Duke of Norfolk
Weston Park, Earl of Bradford	

Fishing

The etiquette which surrounds shooting is not so apparent in fishing circles. There are one or two *faux pas* to be made such as fishing in another man's water which can lead to incandescent rage in the fisherman ahead of you. This will result in much shouting, waving of arms and tangled lines — which will scare off shoals of trout and ruin your day.

Clothing, like for shooting, must be dull and women are not encouraged to wear perfume. Those tweed hats with flys stuck all over them are regarded as somewhat non-U and are usually worn by young men with open top sports-cars — in order to make a subtle statement that they are not totally 'towners'.

In Scotland, where much attention is paid to protocol, it is considered pretty dreadful if you do not offer your gillie a nip from your flask and he should be called by either his Christian or surname never 'gillie'. His advice should always be taken — to ignore it is foolish as he probably knows the river far better than you do.

Say fishing not angling as that conjures up the picture of men crouched under golf umbrellas besides filled in gravel pits. The 'aristocratic' fisherman never uses worms to catch salmon (and if he did he would be regarded as nothing better than his bait), but is an expert on dry and wet flies and has no trouble tying them even when his hands are blue with cold.

Rivers

IN	OUT
Grimesta (the most exclusive seven miles of salmon fishing almost anywhere) in the Outer Hebrides, Lewis	Thames (despite attempts to bring back life to the river it is still only fit for boating)
	Dee
Brora, Sutherlandshire	Test (a stockbroker's river)

The Tweed
The Spey
Oykell
Eden, Cumberland
Usk
Avon, above Salisbury
(top half)
Nadder
Park (in the early part of
the season only)

Tay (expensive but
unfashionable)
Wharfe, Yorkshire
Itchen

Hunts

IN
Quorn
The Pytchley
Belvoir
Scarteen
High Peak Harriers
Beaufort
County Galway

OUT
Eridge
Heythrop
Portman
Four Barrow
Cottesmore
Wentbridge

13

Knowledge

WITH his increase in affluence the pretender is often tempted to purchase a car which he feels will enhance his social position. Nothing could be further from the truth. As Douglas Sutherland has pointed out, the gentleman does not drive around in a status symbol. Although he may be the possessor of a Rolls Royce it would certainly never be a new one. It is more likely to be approaching vintage status and probably worth more cleaned-up, off the road, and in a museum rather than conveying its owner to the shops and back. In appearance the Rolls will be dusty (if kept in town), and scratched and mud splattered if stabled in the country. The smell of new leather will have long vanished. The adage goes that the only gentleman in a Rolls is the chauffeur—this, of course, could be social jealousy by those who cannot afford such a car. It is perhaps best that anyone not sure of the ways of society leave them to be snapped up by Americans, Swiss and those departing for tax exile. Such an attitude will do no end of good for Britain's problematic balance of payments.

Number plates are another giveaway. The only excuse for transferring one from an old car to a new is because its owner, being totally innumerate, does not have the ability to remember a combination of seven figures and letters. When a JOE 1, S I D, FAST 120, TOY 2 or NFM 50 passes you by it is clear that the hand of *nouveau riche* has been at work.

The unskilful with an *embarras de richesse* will head for Jack Barclay and order a Camargue in Canary Yellow in the hope that attention will focus on him. No

A new Rolls—not the car to enhance the social position.

one of discernment will be seen dead in the thing and the
once proud owner will have made a black.

Cars

A WISE PURCHASE	AN UNWISE PURCHASE
Jeeps (very in)	Range Rovers in town
Aston Martin Lagonda	Mini Mokes
BMWs (all)	MG Midget
Beetle Convertibles	MGB
Ferrari (all)	Mustangs
Rover	Rolls Royce
Alfa Romeo GTV	Iso Grifo
Mini 1000	Alfa Sud
Renault 5 (for women)	Mini and Mini Cooper (v. 60s)
Bristol	Reliant Scimitar
Alvis	Marina
Porsche	Talbot Sunbeam
Saab	Jaguar (as it ever was)
DBS (as driven by Prince Charles)	Daimler (a Jag by any other name)
Morgan	Cortina
Mercedes	Ford Escort, Granada, Cortina (unless provided by the office)
Zil	Beach Buggy (passé)
Fiat Mirafiori	Lamborghini
Opel (most)	Lotus
Panther	Triumph TR7
	Triumph Spitfire
	Triumph Toledo
	Simca

Holidays

Summer

IN	OUT
Penang	Greek Islands
Ibizia	Majorca
Pamplona (for running bulls)	Rio (for carnival)
	Sardinia
Turkey	Monte Carlo
Salzburg	Venice (because it smells)
Dalmatian Islands	St. Tropez (not what it was)
Japan	
Peking	Canaries
Dordogne	Daytona Beach
Jura	Bahamas
Lanzarote	Long Beach, California
Ascot week	Falkland Islands (unless
Southern Italy	you like lamb and mutton and lamb etc.)

Winter

IN	OUT
Megève	Mustique (being (developed)
Sri Lanka	
Corcheval	Reykjavik
Tijuana	Hawaii
Bakony Forest, Hungary	Bali
Ulan Bator, Mongolia	Jamaica
Gstaad (for those who prefer *après ski*)	Seychelles
	The Lake District
Australia	Russia (no fun without sun)
New Guinea	
Kenya	St. Moritz
Aspen, Colorado	Isola 2000
Venice (as it doesn't smell)	South Africa
	Hong Kong
On a Col. Blashford Snell	Nepal

expedition
Uganda (for the wild life)
Barbados
Cape Verde Islands
Dominica, Windward
   Islands
Sabah or Sarawak,
   Malaysia
Wallis and Futuna
   Islands, Melanesia
Erewhon (for literary
   persons)

On a Sir Ranolph
   Twisleton-Wykeham-
   Fiennes expedition as
   they are more than
   dangerous
Iran
Nicaragua
Toto

Knowledge

Nicknames to drop—but know who they are before using them.
Brookie
Boofy
Bubbles
Bobo
Rollo
Piggy
Bear
Piranah
Pongo
Blashers
Chalky
Stoker
Demi-monde
Goldilocks
The pope
Var
Jaws
Seducer of the valleys
Sharon
Phyllis

. . . "saw Pongo at Bubble's bash and Stoker told me it's
all on between Hottie and James."

Fog
Thoroughly unscrupulous
Porchy
Hottie
Sunny

The world of music

Opera Houses

IN	OUT
Scottish Opera	Glyndebourne Festival
La Scala, Milan	(full of people who go
English National	to be seen and to pop
Metropolitan, New York	champagne corks in the
Bavarian State	garden)
	Bayreuth
	Salzburg Festival
	Paris

Singers

Kiri Te Kanawa	Luciano Pavarotti
Frederica Von Stade	Joan Sutherland
Silvia Sass	Placido Domingo
Jose Carreras	Dietrich Fischer-Dieskau
Ileana Cotrubas	Sherrill Milnes
Renato Bruson	Beverley Sills

Musicians

Gidon Kremer (violin)	Vladimir Horowitz (piano)
Lynn Harrell (cello)	Yehudi Menuhin (violin)
Tokyo Quartet	Daniel Barenboim (piano)
Emil Gilels (piano)	Pinchas Zukerman (violin)
Emanuel Ax (piano)	Mstislav Rostropovich
Kyung Wha Chung	(cello)
(violin)	Amadeus Quartet
Itzhak Perlman (violin)	James Galway (flute)

Orchestras

Vienna Philharmonic	New York Philharmonic
London Philharmonic	London Symphony
Los Angeles Philharmonic	Orchestra
Dresden Staatskapelle	Academy of St. Martin's
Leningrad Philharmonic	Philadelphia Orchestra
Boston Symphony	Cleveland Orchestra

Conductors

Carlos Kleiber	André Previn
Klaus Tennstedt	Zubin Mehta
Claudio Abbado	Riccardo Muti
James Levine	Pierre Boulez
Karl Bohm	Herbert von Karajan
Eugen Jochum	Lorin Maazel
Gennadi Rozhdestvensky	Daniel Barenboim
	Leonard Bernstein

Reading

Right reading is essential.

IN	OUT
Nigel Dempster's Mail Diary (none more essential than this)	Peterborough, Daily Telegraph
	All motoring magazines
William Hickey (important when above has an off day)	Brides
	House and Garden
	Private Eye (Grovel etc.)
Harpers and Queen	What's On—except for Oliver Hush on Theatre gossip
Vogue (for women)	
Frizz for photographs	
London Index for Timothy Swallow	The Lady (unless you want a nanny)
Ritz magazine	Life & Country Life (unless grouse counts are important to you)
People magazine from America	

The Times (?) court circular, births, deaths etc. in absentia the same in the Daily Telegraph

Londoner's Diary, Evening Standard

Richard Compton Miller, Evening News

Lady Olga Maitland's diary, Sunday Express

The Tatler

People and Places, Yorkshire Post

Sandra Harris on Thames at Six

NOW!

Which helicopter?

IN	OUT
Jet Ranger	Hughes 500 (the back seat is uncomfortable)
Long Ranger	Aloutte

Charters

IN	OUT
Alan Mann	British Airways
Air Hanson (ask for the Long Ranger with the cocktail cabinet)	Bristow

Which Plane?

IN	OUT
Boeing 737	DC 10
Grumman Gulfstream 111	Lockheed Jet Star
Tiger Moth (for the modest)	Concorde (anti-social in times of oil economy)
Cessna Citation	Jumbo (too ostentatious for private use)
	Corvette
	Lear Jet

(109)

Cheque Books to carry

IN	OUT
Trustees Savings Bank	Coutts (not exclusive any more)
The Bank of England (exclusive because they open few private accounts)	National Westminster
	Barclays
	Lloyds
American Express Bank	Midland (except for farmers to whom it is said they are well disposed)
Grindleys (mainly for colonials)	
Hill Samuel (they have a few personal accounts for rich businessmen)	Bank Du Rhone
	Allied Irish
United Bank of Kuwait (a friend once spilled salad dressing on his cheque book and everyone thought he was in oil)	Williams and Glyn (except if you have a Child cheque book)
Hoares	

14

When it all gets too much:-

Mind Improvement Therapy and Growth

IN	OUT
Tai Chi Chuan (British Lam-Rin Centre)	Utopian Thought (idealistic)
Gestalt Therapy	Silva method of mind control
Carl Jung (fashionable for signs and symbolism)	Postural Integration Foot Massaure
Gurdjieff and Ouspensky Centres	Alexander Technique
Pre-natal foot therapy	The Institute of Psychotherapy
R.D. Laing	Social Studies (for interperson psychoanalytic approaches and humanistic approaches)
	THF Dancing Bodymind
	Transcendental Meditation
	EST
	Tushita
	Sigmund Freud

Death

The totally dedicated socialite, having pursued his hedonistic desires all through life, is unlikely to break any human longevity records—which brings us to the final chapter. Snobbery is with us to the day we die and the amount of interest raised at one's passing is indicative of the success achieved during our earthly existence.

Modern society has little respect or interest in death. While our Victorian forebears were obsessed with death — middle aged women were always at some stage of mourning — we tend to avoid the subject which we find embarrassing, and have a preference to talk about sex, a topic which the Victorians regarded as taboo.

One can only hope (depending on the size of individual egos) that our final journey up the aisle will be watched by gently weeping relations, friends, ex-wives and lovers. Only the excessively egotistical will wish for books to be written, statues to be erected and streets named after them.

For the most part a sympathetic obituary, written by a friend, in The Times would suffice and a quiet funeral followed by burial in the family mausoleum, or for the more dramatic a ritual scattering of ashes at sea.

"What's this IN AND OUT book everyone's reading."